LIGHTNING BOLT BOOKS

T0015855

Dangerous Wildfires

Lola Schaefer

Lerner Publications • Minneapolis

Thank you, Jason
Thistlethwaite,
University of
Waterloo

Lerner Publications Company
An imprint of Lerner Publishing Group, Inc.
241 First Avenue North
Minneapolis, MN 55401 USA

For reading levels and more information, look up this title at www.lernerbooks.com.

Main body text set in Billy Infant Regular. Typeface provided by SparkType.

Library of Congress Cataloging-in-Publication Data

Names: Schaefer, Lola M., 1950- author.
Title: Dangerous wildfires / Lola Schaefer.
Description: Minneapolis : Lerner Publications, [2022] | Series: Lightning bolt books—Earth in danger | Includes bibliographical references and index. | Audience: Ages 6-9 | Audience: Grades 2-3 | Summary: "Climate change is making wildfires worse, and it's important to know how to stay safe. Read about what causes a fire, what makes it grow, and what happens when fire makes people leave their homes"—Provided by publisher.
Identifiers: LCCN 2021016796 (print) | LCCN 2021016797 (ebook) | ISBN 9781728441412 (library binding) | ISBN 9781728447988 (paperback) | ISBN 9781728444871 (ebook)
Subjects: LCSH: Wildfires—Juvenile literature.
Classification: LCC SD421.23 .S33 2022 (print) | LCC SD421.23 (ebook) | DDC 634.9/618—dc23

LC record available at https://lccn.loc.gov/2021016796
LC ebook record available at https://lccn.loc.gov/2021016797

Manufactured in the United States of America
1-49912-49755-7/26/2021

Table of Contents

Wildfires Burn

Lightning strikes dry grass.
The wind blows and sparks fly.
A fire begins.

Flames race across the land. Dry shrubs and trees burn. Soon the wildfire is out of control.

Dry plants help wildfires grow.

A wildfire may burn forests, grasslands, or swamps. A ground fire burns plant roots.

Some grasses have deep roots and quickly grow back after a fire.

A surface fire burns dried plants on the ground. A crown fire burns leaves higher off the ground.

How Wildfires Begin

Climate change warms Earth. This dries out the land and plants. Dry plants are fuel for wildfires.

More wildfires happen when the climate warms. These fires may be larger, last longer, and cause more damage.

O₂

OXYGEN

HEAT

FUEL

Fire needs oxygen, heat,
and fuel to start and burn.
Removing any one of these
will put out the fire.

The heat that starts a wildfire can be natural, such as a lightning strike. Or the heat can be caused by humans, such as sparks from fireworks.

In 2018, fireworks caused about 19,500 fires in the US.

Dangerous Wildfires

In 2020, more than fifty-eight thousand wildfires burned in the United States. Some of these burned for months.

A wildfire makes the air hot and polluted. Smoke causes people to cough and their eyes to burn.

Smoke is a combination of gases and particles. A particle is something that is very small.

Wind can change the direction and intensity of wildfires.

A wildfire can change directions quickly. Large wildfires can burn buildings. Sometimes people need to flee their homes.

Wildfires can also do good. Their heat opens some pine cones so seeds can grow. After a burn, sunlight can reach new plants on the ground.

This pine cone has seeds in it. A fire's heat melts the cone and releases the seeds.

Staying Safe

Practice leaving your home safely with two different plans. Choose a place where your family can meet if you get separated.

Your evacuation kit should include a first aid kit in case someone gets hurt.

Make an evacuation kit. Pack extra clothing, face coverings, and a flashlight. Store extra water and food to carry with you.

If you see a fire, call 911. Firefighters are trained in putting out fires.

Learn emergency phone numbers. If wildfires are near you, stay close to home. Listen to the news, and leave if asked.

Wildfires are natural disasters. But we can prevent some of them. Never play with matches. Only adults should use fire, and only when conditions aren't too dry. Be safe!

This sign warns of high fire risk. People should not have campfires when fire danger is high.

FIRE DANGER
HIGH
TODAY!

I Survived a Wildfire

In April 2017, lightning started a fire in the Okefenokee Swamp. Grady Allbritton watched winds push the wildfire closer to his town of Saint George, Georgia. Gray-and-white ash covered cars, homes, and roads. Allbritton helped prepare and deliver meals to first responders who fought the fire. Thanks in part to their hard work, Allbritton and his town survived.

Wildfire Facts

- At least 80 percent of all wildfires are started by people.

- Fire tornadoes, or fire whirls, occur when superhot dry air shoots upward 100 to 1,000 feet (30 to 304 m) in a swirling motion at speeds of 70 to 90 miles (113 to 145 km) an hour.

- Between 2019 and 2020, wildfires called bushfires burned for nine months in parts of Australia. They destroyed 72,000 square miles (186,479 sq. km) of land and thousands of homes.

Glossary

climate change: long-term changes in global temperature due to human activity

emergency: a sudden and dangerous situation

evacuation: leaving a dangerous area

fuel: a source of energy

oxygen: a colorless gas found in the air

polluted: dirty

prevent: to stop something from happening

Learn More

Britannica Kids: Wildfire
https://kids.britannica.com/students/article
/wildfire/629045

Gagliardi, Sue. *California Wildfires*. Lake Elmo, MN:
Focus Readers, 2020.

Kiddle: Wildfire Facts for Kids
https://kids.kiddle.co/Wildfire

Pettiford, Rebecca. *Wildfires*. Minneapolis:
Bellwether, 2020.

Schaefer, Lola. *Dangerous Droughts*. Minneapolis:
Lerner Publications, 2022.

Smokey for Kids: Preventing Wildfires
https://smokeybear.com/en/smokey-for-kids
/preventing-wildfires

Index

Photo Acknowledgments

Image credits: Kevin Cass/Shutterstock.com, p. 4; mironov/Shutterstock.com, p. 5; Lumppini/
Shutterstock.com, p. 6; Alin Brotea/Shutterstock.com, p. 7; Kent Raney/Shutterstock.com,
p. 8; Toa55/Shutterstock.com, p. 9; VectorMine/Shutterstock.com, p. 10; Greta Gabaglio/
Shutterstock.com, p. 11; Matt Gush/Shutterstock.com, p. 12; Anton27/Shutterstock.com,
p. 13; Dmytro Gilitukha/Shutterstock.com, p. 14; A.Luna/Shutterstock.com, p. 15; Serhii Krot/
Shutterstock.com, p. 16; Roger Brown Photography/Shutterstock.com, p. 17; McLittle Stock/
Shutterstock.com, p. 18; Natalia Bratslavsky/Shutterstock.com, p. 19.

Cover image: Christian Roberts-Olsen/Shutterstock.com.